101 Lead Generation Strategies That Work

Ultra-Low Cost

Sales and Marketing Strategies

for Small Businesses

By Sharif George

Parvus Magna Press

5 Ambleside Close, Leyton, London, E10 5RU
Email: sharif@pmpress.uk
Website: www.pmpress.uk

© 2013 by Sharif George

Sharif George has asserted his right under the copyright, designs and patents act 1988, to be identified as author of this work.

All rights reserved. No part of this publication may be reproduced, stored in a retrieval system, or transmitted, in any form or by any means, electronic, mechanical, photocopying, recording or otherwise, without the prior permission of the publisher or the Copyright Licensing Agency.

FIRST EDITION – March 2016

British Library Cataloguing in Publication Data
A catalogue record and a copy of this book are available from the British Library

ISBN: 978-1-910372-03-6

Parvus Magna Press publishes limited run and niche interest books in the UK. If you would like to see your book in print, please email your manuscript to sharif@pmpress.uk

Contents

Contents 3
Introduction 5
Section 1 – The Basics 7
Section 2 – What do you sell? 37
Section 3 – Networking Strategies 47
Section 4 – Website Strategies 73
Section 5 - Real Media 95
Section 6 – Phone Campaigns 113
Section 7 – Other Ideas 121
Section 8 - Exhibitions 129
Section 9 – Google Stuff 159
Section 10 – Social Media 175
Section 11 - Email Marketing 180

Introduction

Over the years, I have had the privilege to get involved with hundreds of small businesses and I have met thousands of great entrepreneurs.

The one thing that all of these incredible people have in common is their desire to see their business or their idea grow.

The fact you are browsing this books suggests to me that this what you need too!

After nearly 20 years' working in the front line of sales and marketing, I thought I would write a follow-up book to my first book The Entrepreneurs Guide to Email Marketing, which is now in its third edition.

The secret of any successful business comes down to a very simple bottom line – the bottom line!

If you don't have cash in the business, it will fail. I know this. I have run 4 businesses and each has had its own financial challenges and the key to overcoming those challenges was always get more sales. Get more money coming in!

Sales does not always equal cash, but the two are so closely aligned that there is barely a hairs breadth between them.

Therefore, that is what this book is about – how to turn your business into a cash generating sales engine!

Detailed here are 115 low cost and free lead generation ideas that you can use to really accelerate your business.

Section 1 – The Basics

The basics of a sales campaign can be boiled down to three simple pieces of advice.

Firstly, plan your campaign

Secondly, do what you planned

Third, Change the plan!

Your planning stage is important because here you can arrange for all the tools you use to work together to your advantage.

Focus everything on a single clear message – but more about that below.

1. What do you Sell and Who to?

The Sales Engine Works on the principle that consistent and focused attention on sales and marketing brings results.

We know that as we have seen these methods work with thousands of businesses just like yours. These powerful tools are designed to massively increase your lead generation and sales conversions. With these tools, hundreds of business people just like you have changed their businesses ideas into cash generating assets.

One of the real keys behind these tools is getting the right automated systems in place to make sure that you can scale your efforts.

Core to the Sales Engine is the idea that everything, is centred on your technology system, everything is recorded into your CRM (Customer Relationship Management System), every phone call, every email, every PPC campaign click and every bit of web activity. The main thrust of the Sales Engine campaign is TEST and MEASURE and record.

The Sales Engine works because it is focused on Engagement rather than broadcasting. Your focus is going to be on finding out what engages the client and then repeating that engagement process for that client consistently until they buy.

Here is an example. In our LinkedIn PPC section we suggest personally targeting your networking contacts on LinkedIn with a customised 121 campaign. However, what if your client never logs into LinkedIn – then the campaign is wasted.

> *Simon was trying to get hold of a local clothes shop owner via LinkedIn in order to start a conversation about changing wholesaler.*
>
> *Simon started with telephone calls and then moved onto emails and then even he even showed her custom LinkedIn ads – she never clicked a link.*

> *Simon met with one of the Sales Engine consultants and we suggested he change his campaign to Facebook – guess what the shop owner called within three days!*

If Simon had continued to push LinkedIn and emails at the client he may never have go the business, by measuring the engagement he was having with the client we were able to change our approach to match the leads frame of reference.

The job of the Sales Engine consultant is to help you find the best CRM and automation systems that matches your business and help you set it up and integrate it with your marketing exercises so that you can record your client interactions and automate as much of the marketing as you can.

2. The Four M's of Marketing

How many "M"s in Marketing? Four! That is right the four M's of marketing are Market, Message, Media and Measure!

M = Market – Who is your ideal client or networking contact? Your ideal client may be different from the ideal person you network with, especially if what you sell is a low priced item or service.

If you are a Mortgage broker then spend your time networking finding people who can introduce you to potential clients, rather than just getting potential clients from within the network.

Who are the potential introducers to your business?

> *We were helping a local electrician with their marketing and one of their services was to replace fuse boards, landlords often had to replace the units to comply with safety legislation.*
>
> *So our Question was: How do we get to landlords?*
>
> *Through Estate Agents – but they are notoriously hard to deal with. These are busy sales people and they are not interested in maintenance and repair and artisans/tradespeople. So how do we draw them into our lair and get them to refer us to landlord?*
>
> *Well once we knew whom we needed to speak to, the next stage was simple – what do Estate Agents want to hear?*

With the right systems in place you can segment your messages and effort to ensure that the right person gets the right message.

M = Message – Who you speak to is important will define how you speak to them. Our Estate agents certainly don't really care if you are a plumber or electrician who is local. Mostly they won't even give you time of day, so you have to find a way of gaining their attention.

We harnessed the message with a methodology that we repeated until we got the response we needed.

Our message was "save time with us" we wrapped in a message that "we would take care of everything" and "leave you, the agent, free to sell". The agents by spending less time on maintenance would have more time to sell. This simple message led to "make more money". We coupled this with a commission structure which meant that they agent was able to make a little bit from each referral.

We kept the message simple "we are electricians who specialise in fuse boards, we can save you time by dealing with the whole job direct with the landlord, and we give you a commission if you refer us"

Of course, we turned the message around when we presented it to the Estate Agent. "When you need a new fuse board fitted with the minimal hassle and delay, call Tom" – followed by the offer of commission.

M = Method – Whether you use leaflets or postcards, emails or telephone calls, brochure or website this is the "how" of our equation.

With our Electrician, he walked into the estate agents at least once a month and asked for the business. Leaving behind a postcard that promised a healthy commission on the first referral and a promise that the agent would not have to get deeply involved.

"Don't worry, leave it all to me"

The method was to produce the maximum possible impact with the Agents. Agents often are very personable, friendly and people focused – they have to be or they could not sell property.

Therefore, to try to attract agents via email and a website was never going to be as effective as turning up. Our method allowed the electrician (the salesman) to get to know the agents and through that relationship – build rapport into business.

So find the method that works best for your Market and allows you to deliver your message effectively.

If your market is best connected with in person, then find a message that can be communicated in person and affirmed easily via other methods.

Market should drive message should drive method. But they all serve the fourth M

M = Measure – With the system in place we set about measuring the response we got from the estate agents. Knowing our market meant we knew we had to make referring as easy as possible. The first thing we did was set up a dedicated telephone number for the campaign that had campaign diagnostics built into it. Every time someone called on that number, we knew the call had come through the Estate Agents Campaign.

Secondly, we had a microsite set up so that we could measure interest. This was also integrated to the CRM (Customer Relationship Management) system so that if a click came through from an outbound email – we knew who had visited and we made sure we "popped in" a few days later to say hi.

Thirdly, we made sure we recorded every visit in the system and the result of the "meeting" recorded too.

> *We found to our delight that about 25% of the estate agents we visited a third time, responded with positive signals and by the time we got the fifth visit – they were referring clients to us regularly.*

The cost of installing a new fuse board is about £800 - £1,500 and is one of the most profitable things this firm does, but they didn't just get fuse boards, they proved themselves reliable and so got a lot of other jobs too. Soon the agents were asking them to do minor repairs and major rewiring jobs as well.

During the campaign, the measure element was vital to know how we were doing and what sort of conversions we could expect. By understanding the dynamics of the method, we were able to predict the results when we moved the methodology onto a new area.

Lifetime value of the client. I was working with a Hotel recently trying to increase their income from locals in their restaurant and bar. One of the greatest difficulties was explaining this thing called "lifetime value of the client".

How much you spend on client acquisition has to be directly related, in some way to this figure.

For example:- Our electrician was willing to spend up to £400 to acquire a new client because they had worked out (with our help) that the average lifetime value of the client would be something in the region of £50 - £100k.

Part of the job of the measurement part of marketing is to track that figure and track the effectiveness of the marketing – are we making money.

3. The Secret of Sales – What do you see

So having dealt with the basics of the four "m"s of marketing, perhaps we should have a look at the secret of sales. The secret ingredient that makes the difference between a good and an excellent sales campaign.

The Sales process is really not complex, it is just like the funnel shown below, you try and engage people and make them aware of your product or service and then convince them to buy from you.

You will meet people, either online or offline and then feed those who would buy from you into the top of a funnel.

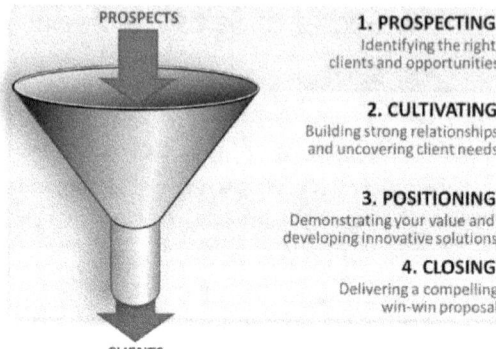

You then cultivate the relationships with these people by using a number of tools, including telemarketing, email marketing, newsletters and advertising to nurture them into a position where they ask for a quote.

The process relies heavily on numbers, more people in the top always means more people out the bottom.

To a certain degree this is in fact the full complexity of the sales process any salesman can be successful if they can get the numbers up.

> *It's simply this – if you ask enough people to buy from you – someone will.*

Part of my job in this book is about making that process more efficient and increasing the net result. We will do that by introducing an element into the marketing mix that is often missed out – YOU!

You may have heard this before – but people buy people. People buy from people they know, like and trust.

However, people **refer** to people they know, like, trust and support or advocate. This is very important for your networking. You are aiming at producing advocates, not just customers – raging fans – not just clients.

Networking

Over the years I have built a network of fans, people who will refer business to me regardless of whether they actually buy from me or not.

Some people know us really well, they like us enough and they trust us. These are our inner circle; often the trust is mutual and often based on experience (though not always so).

These people will buy from us if they have the need to.

Then there are those who have not quite made that leap of trust yet. They know us and like us but, as yet, have no basis to trust us. They may buy if there is sufficient pain and we are the ones holding the pill but they will not necessarily buy through choice.

Then there are those who know us, have not yet formed enough of an opinion one way or another about liking us and quite probably have no view on liking or trusting. Once again, pain may cause this person to come to you but it is less likely.

The Sales Engine is designed to help you draw people through the first two rings as quickly as you can so that they sit in the central Trust ring. Once there, your prospect is more likely to buy from you. Actually more likely to come to you first.

Over the years I have found the easiest sales are those where I have been approached by the prospect to resolve a problem or issue for them.

Where all the relationship work has already been worked out and where we are already working inside that centre circle.

A lot of your work over the next few months will be about building up these kinds of relationships with your network so that you can increase the "walk-in" sales. In retail, it is known that more customers walk in through an open door, than through a closed one. Your job in networking is to open the door!

With the Sales Engine – everything in this process is to draw people into your inner circle. Everything must be tested, measured, recorded and then, if it works, repeated.

4. The Sales Plan

Your Sales plan is your map; it helps you stay focused and serves as the focal point of all your activity. The Plan is not a finished document, it never will be and with the marketplace changing like it does almost daily, you will need to adjust and rework your sales plan accordingly.

1) Attraction – is getting your product into the radar of your prospects. Remember the more prospects you feed into your sales funnel, the more sales are likely to come out of the other end.

   Unlike the tradition thought that more is better, we like to focus on getting more of the right type of prospects.

If you sell baby car seats you are not going to get many takers in the 50+ age bracket so why bombard them with emails.

Many people shy away from spending money on prospecting, don't! This is the cheapest part of your marketing plan if done right and although you will not convert 100% of prospects, if you get the mix right, you can get a very high conversion rate.

2) Development – The development phase is all about establishing a rapport with your prospects in a way that draws them in towards the centre of your circles.

The development phase is usually the longest part of the process. Using whatever tools you have at your disposal to keep in touch with the prospects.

Part of the process should try and gain useful intelligence about your prospects needs. The more information you gain at this stage the easier it will become to convert prospects to clients.

3) Close – This happens when your offer can't be resisted, your prospect needs what you're offering or even better desires it – they are on the hook and it is all about the close.

Well perhaps I should have said 4?

4) How are we going to get them to buy again? The biggest marketplace for your services and products is that group of

people you have already sold to. They have spent money with you already; and if all went well, they are right in the centre of the trust ring.

It's my opinion that consultancies do not do enough work in the area of getting their existing customer base to buy again. They leave thousands of sales just sitting there for want of a follow-up call.

Some analysts say that to sell to a new client costs more than 8 times as much as selling to an existing client – why wouldn't you want to sell more to your customers.

OK 5 things

5) Is there a way that you can turn them into income? Is there a subscription model here, is there a way getting

them to buy from you repeatedly?

> Microsoft did this with their Microsoft Office program, they turned the capital income which they would usually receive once every 3 to 5 years to a subscription base where they will get paid more money every year!

6 things then…

6) Actually, we want them to become fans. We want our contacts to become raving fans and refer us repeatedly – we want to turn our clients into a massive network of advocates.

With The Sales Engine, we are happier with fewer well-targeted prospects than masses of untargeted ones – but if we can get masses of targeted ones then we won't complain!

Your Sales Plan will reflect three important differences with traditional sales and marketing plan.

Firstly, it will be sales orientated, not lead orientated – we are not looking for leads we are looking for sales. We will start there and work our way backwards.

> "The road to profitability is paved with credibility. Credibility is something you earn by how you market, where you market, how you treat people, how you act, and your overall level of professionalism. Away from the business arena, the term is street cred, and it's the road to respect."
>
> Jay Conrad Levinson

Secondly, it will be about focused conversations not broadcasting. We are not interested in yelling at prospects, we are interested in inviting them to an intimate conversation which **they want to have**.

> *An example of this was a campaign we ran in Cloudberry a few years back. We knew that a certain subset of our clients were avid skiers. I was talking to a travel agent one day and asked him if he had any outrageous deals on skiing holidays he wanted to sell – he did.*
>
> *We sent an email out to a group of eight prospects offering them a massive discount on a skiing holiday – we made sure they had each other's email address as well. They arranged to all go on this ski trip. I don't ski, so I didn't go with them – but …*
>
> *About 5 months after this email and half of them have either become clients or referred new clients to me.*

> *By understanding what these contacts wanted to hear – I converted them to sales.*
>
> *Oh and by the way with that email, I got 100% read rate and 100% response rate too!*

Thirdly, we are not looking to spend a lot of money! Jay Conrad Levinson is a hero of mine, I love the guerrilla marketing books and highly recommend getting the original book – though it is dated, it has many foundational ideas that we use in the Sales Engine.

Your sales plan needs to include the following sections.

1) How are you going to attract people to talk to you?
2) How are you going to keep their attention?
3) How are you going to convert them into a sale?
4) How are you going to convert them into more sales?

5) How are you going to convert them into income?

5. Be a Guerrilla

To fight the big players in your market sector is going to take a lot more capital than you have to spend. You need to use a method that makes maximum use of your limited resources but gives you the widest possible exposure *to the exact people who need your products.*

Much of what you read here is about niching your activities.

We know that the best prospect list is the one where 100% of the prospects buy your product so that none of your effort is wasted.

Do not fight hard for large marketplaces but find a niche and corner it, smaller market places are easier to cater for than larger. Big Fish little pond!

> "you don't need many. You need only one good one."
>
> Jay Conrad Levinson

Does your product have mass appeal – still market in niches? If you get a large take up in a small niche, it will spread. Also by concentrating on niche marketing messages you are appealing more directly to your buyer's needs.

Even with a broad or mass appeal product using a niche marketing strategy can pay off quickly. If you market your mass-market product at property lawyers in London, you will find that you are able to write a message that is just aimed at one customer type.

6. Be Specific

Another big mistake is trying to market everything you can do. Wicks have all the tools and materials you need to build a house – but they are not known for building houses, they are known as a building material and tools supplier.

Each marketing campaign should be aimed at a single product or service – not all of them – just one. If you are a coach and you do executive coaching, make a product of your services (see below) and then sell that one product on a niche marketing campaign.

You will get business in the other areas if you want it but you water down the effect of your marketing if you water down your message.

> *I recently sat in a networking meeting with a Lawyer who in his 60 seconds started to tell us all the different things that he could do. You know the stuff, Commercial, Litigation, employment, property etc.*

> *Not only did he go over his 60 seconds (and the next persons) he did not get any referrals.*
>
> *However, straight after this meeting, I had a lunch networking group and the lawyer there asked if we knew anyone who needed a new employment contract drawn up.*
>
> *He got 3 referrals.*

Be Specific, I have heard so many examples of people who have asked for specific referrals and got them!

Actually, the main reason for specific is it will speak directly to your potential client's needs – they do not have to think about it. The electrician we spoke about earlier, he only advertised Fuse Board!

> "if you can talk to them about themselves, you'll have their full attention."
>
> Jay Conrad Levinson

7. Start

That's it – start!!

> A journey of a thousand miles starts with just one step.
>
> Chinese Proverb

The journey of sales and marketing success starts with just 1 step.

What that single step is, is down to you.

Section 2 – What do you sell?

One of the major tasks of marketing and sales strategy is figuring out what it is that you actually sell and why it is your clients buy from you.

Mr Charles Revson, co-founder of Revlon (t) knew what it was he sold when he said,

> "In our factory we make cosmetics. In the store we sell hope".

What do you sell and why do people buy from you? When you understand this, you understand the motivation behind why people buy your product then you will easily be able to identify customers and offer them exactly what they are looking for.

If you don't know, ask!

If you already have people that are buying your product and you are not sure why, why not ask them?

Call the client and ask them these three questions, record the answers and you will be surprised at the results.

1) What did/do you buy from us?
2) Why did you choose us?
3) Do you feel that you get good value for money?
4) How could we do better

It's nerve wracking but the results are gold dust and will help you market your business with a real sense of direction.

By the way, if there are customers you want a particular "type" of – then ask them as a group and record their answers separately for a more focused answer.

Record everything, even the telephone calls if you can, this is market intelligence that will make such a huge difference to your marketing because it will give your marketing a definite and predictable direction.

8. You do not have a USP

Well OK you just might have a USP but it is very rare that it is in fact unique.

This idea was the starting point of niche marketing and niche sales several years ago and although it is no longer very valid, it is useful to keep as an exercise.

Because it helps you refine your offering and your marketing will only gain traction and attraction thereby.

Use the answers to the second question to help fuel your thinking about your USP.

How do you find your USP?

The easiest way is to call up your top 20 customers and ask them three questions.

1) Why did you buy from me?
2) What made me different from the rest?
3) What keeps you using me?

Some people use USP to mean Unique Selling Proposition.

Your proposition is a combination of factors, your personality, your product or service – the combination of services etc.

Great customer service is not a USP – banks even claim that, I have never met anyone who said they were unfriendly and I haven't heard someone try and tell me they do a bad job....

The USP can be a powerful tool if you have something unique, use it carefully to maximise your message and your results.

9. Do you understand your Clients Buying Motivation?

In recent years, sales psychologists have been doing a lot of research into buyer motivation, they discovered that the real motivation for buying goods and services can often be distilled down to the ideas "to resolve a problem" or "satisfy a need". This is sometimes called buyer motivation.

"Don't lose your memories – backup your photos now" is an emotional fear trigger and fear is the buying motivation for this backup product. This type of emotional trigger is called "away from motivation". Away from motivation moves a person away from a fear towards safety.

"Share those happy memories put your photos online" is definitely more positive, not necessarily a more effective strategy though. This is "towards motivation" it motivates a person to go towards something that they find desirable.

> "What a fool man is, when he comes to the last ditch, not to spend the last farthing to satisfy the inner man before he goes out to fight a battle with wits"
>
> G K Chesterton

Buyer motivation is in short, the emotional lever that causes someone to buy your product or enlist your service. People are more likely to spend money on something if it fulfils a want or a need, it is how you connect your product or service to the wants or needs of your customer.

In order to find your buyer motivation, you have to understand your existing customers. Why did they buy from you? What issues did you resolve for them, what emotions were they experiencing before they found you and of course what emotions they felt when you took over – That will give you input on both away from and towards motivation.

10. Defining your product

Define your product using features and benefits. Features are what your product does – benefits are why that is important.

You know what your product is. This doesn't necessarily mean that your customer will understand why they should purchase your product or engage your services. If your product is not fully defined and explained, your customer might not fully understand the value of what you are selling—and that means they won't know why they should buy it.

Defining your product is all about explaining the value of what you offer, whether it is a product or a service. This is done through a two-fold approach: discussing features and explaining benefits.

An example, your feature as a consultant is that you use a tried and tested methodology, but the benefit is that the client can trust your advice because it reduces the risk to the client. This means the client feels safer.

Features should be listed but you should always sell the benefits.

If you look at just about any standard product description, you will see a list of "features." This is a detailed account of what your product can do, what it is made of, who designed it, etc.

The easiest exercise to get this information is to list your features in a single column and then as yourself about each feature "So what?"

> *20 years'*
> *experience is a*
> *feature – So What –*
> *I Know what I am*
> *doing – So What –*
> *You can have*

confidence in me. Confidence is the benefit of 20 years of experience.

Our Engine is 20% more efficient – is a feature – So What – You can save money. Saving money is a benefit.

Money back guarantee – So What – No Risk. Lack of risk is a benefit!

Every feature should be paired with at least one benefit. Explaining the benefits of each feature helps you to understand your marketing message, you may not use all of the benefits (though I would always recommend you do somewhere), but the more you have the more reasons you give the clients to buy.

Section 3 – Networking

If you don't meet and talk to people your sales and marketing will fall short.

What many marketers forget is that the whole purpose of marketing is to drive people to buy. Too often you will have social media marketers look at "engagement metrics" or "social networking reach" and declare their campaigns a success.

What makes a campaign successful is whether it drives people into a buying decision that ends with the client parting with some money in your direction – don't get me wrong – it's all about the cash.

Networking produces a source of warmed up contacts that can be mined to find sales. Without a broad association, your consulting business really will not sell.

11. The Sales Engine Networking Plan

In our opinion, any lead generation that does not involve networking in some form is likely to underperform. Remember, people buy people more than they buy products or services.

In a recent poll commissioned by The Sales Engine[i], we discovered that about 60% of customers who bought from Business Coaches, did not really know what they bought:-

- 44% Bought because the Coach seemed to know what they were doing
- 18% Just liked the coach
- 27% were looking for something specific – the coach said they could provide
- 11% Knew exactly what they signed up for

The scary thing about these statistics is that most of the users made a decision because they knew the coach – the coach "sold to them" they did not go out to buy from the coach. In other words, they met the coach and liked the coach enough to buy from them – **even though they did not actually know what the coach was selling.**

Would those 60% of coaches have that business if they had not got out, met the client, and got along with them?

For the last 12 years, we have been studying what does and does not work in networking and we have discovered a methodology that is guaranteed to work if you use it properly.

This plan can be amended and customised to suit your way of doing things, your tone of voice or your methodology - remember it takes 7 interactions to build trust sufficient for someone to look seriously at what you are offering.

Our Mission is for the people we meet networking to get to know us well enough to buy what we are selling – even if they don't understand what it is!

12. Networking Breakfasts

There are several groups in the UK that we have found particularly powerful; no 1 has to be BNI simply because the whole premise of BNI is referrals.

I earned £8,000 within my first 2 months of BNI in a small chapter that did not have a technical power team – how much more can you make if you find the right group.

This is our number one lead strategy, because it is perhaps the most powerful of all the strategies that we are going to give you, especially if you service the B2B[ii] or B2E[iii] service space. We have seen this strategy work for businesses as diverse as Rat Catchers and Florists.

When used in conjunction with a powerful marketing tool like vTiger or SugarCRM and LinkedIn Marketing this strategy is amazingly powerful.

Breakfast groups typically meet weekly or fortnightly and what makes this work is the continuity of contact. If you read back to our Electrician, it took between five and eight visits for his estate agents campaign to get off the ground.

Most weekly breakfast groups will work because of the acceleration in relationship building. However, there is more to building the relationship than just turning up at the breakfast.

Another group worth considering is 4 Networking, although they do not have a referral bias, their groups are often vibrant and diverse, unlike BNI they allow multiple people from the same discipline into the room.

With informal groups like 4 Networking, your follow-up process has to be very tight or it will not work.

Another great reason to sign up to 4N is they allow you to visit all their groups once you are a member and of course the nice thing about that is it can accelerate the process because other members of your home group are doing the same thing.

13. Networking Lunches

We have separated these because as a rule they work differently, the networking lunch is usually centred around more of a round table/mastermind session that allows members at the table to raise current business issues and allows the table to make suggestions to help move the issue on.

Networking lunches tend to meet monthly and if you combine this strategy with Networking Breakfasts as well as LinkedIn and a CRM you can start to generate some good leads from them.

However, as these meetings are usually less frequent it does take a lot longer to get through the process of building relationships – I would say that if you are meeting people monthly then you are looking at about 6 months or more before the relationships are mature enough to start providing quality business.

As a tip, use your breakfast meeting to find out about lunch meetings, this means you will accelerate your relationship with the person who invites you to lunch and you will find there will be overlaps in terms of people with your other groups – this is a good thing because you are nurturing relationships.

14. Evening Networking

These tend to be bigger events and more informal, perhaps the best known are those run by the local chambers of commerce. However, there are plenty of evening meetings run off the meetup.com platform as well.

Evening events can be most useful when used in combination with a good CRM system. Although the temptation is to get as many cards as you can from the room. Aim instead for a number of "good" conversations. I reckon on 15 minutes as a good rule of thumb. 10 minutes is too short a time to make an impact.

Whenever I am going to attend an evening event, I always scan the guest list to find people I already know. I then use the evening to "bump into them" and renew or refresh the acquaintance. This not only helps the people I know to feel more comfortable at the event, it also adds one onto the 7 interactions I need to move them into the position where if they need my services they are likely to call me.

Note: With all networking – don't talk about yourself, talk about the other person, find out what they do and who they do it for and – be interested in them. They will leave feeling you are the most wonderful widget consultant in the world and you will leave fully prepared to refer people on if you find them…

15. 1 to 1s Meet for coffee

Over the years I have been networking, I have heard a lot people tell me that networking doesn't work for them. In my experience, however, there are some fundamental rules for networking that if you use them they will massively increase the number of leads that you generate regardless of your business type. I personally think networking can work for anybody.

This is the first of these rules:- Meet people for coffee. This is perhaps the most important reason for going networking, not only do you get to meet new people, tell them about your business (see the note above) you also have the opportunity to get a face to face focused meeting with them.

Traditionally you would fight tooth and nail to get an appointment with a decision maker and here they are in front of you, defences down and ready to accept the invitation to coffee! Come on what more encouragement do you need.

There is a great outline on how to have a 1 to 1 with someone available on the www.howdoigetmoresales.com website.

16. Follow Up – Another Coffee?

This may seem very similar to the last section, but it isn't – meeting people for a single 1 to 1 is powerful but what makes it really powerful is you use this occasion to decide whether or not you are going to meet this person again.

If you used The Sale Engine – template for your 1 2 1 you already know a lot about this persons' business and how they get sales. Now you need to ask yourself the question, are they speaking to my clients? Are they a definite lead? Did they express interest in what I am selling?

If the answer to any of these questions is yes and there is no conflict of interest, book a follow up coffee a short while after the first. I usually do this using the following method.

- Find out where they network
- Give them a call and cadge an Invite
- Thank them for the invite and ask them if you can meet up with them before the meeting (I sometimes ask for them to

give me a run-down of what to expect)
- If they are not available, try to get a meeting afterwards.
- If you have followed the method in the networking guide thus far, you are already on meeting 4 out of 7.
- Better if you have used the email methodology I suggested you may well be on interaction 6 or even 7!!

17. Coffee Mornings, PTA's and School Fayres

Well, this one has gone out of fashion a bit but could be a great guerrilla strategy for the right business. If you are a family lawyer or an estate agent this could be the dynamite you are looking for!

Sponsor local community events and increase awareness of your product or service. The secret to being able to measure this type of sponsorship is to use microsites (mini websites), landing pages and tracking telephone numbers.

The difference is you cannot always attend these events but…

Home based business: If you are a parent and involved in the school on a regular basis – offer to host the meeting at your home and when people come over have your wares in evidence.

> *One woman, who ran a custom greetings card business and was on the local PTA – she hosted the meetings at her house and she often had her cards around the kitchen – almost everyone in the PTA bought their greetings cards from her because of this strategy!*

18. Finding Networking Meetings

This is a powerful tool and very much worthwhile thinking about. Where do the other "trades" that speak to your clients gather?

I once attended a web developer's conference and built an alliance with three web developers who have since referred a ton of work to my IT business.

Find out who else speaks to your clients and find out where they meet and meet them there. Guerrilla networking is about going out to your clients and referral network, meeting them on their own ground, and speaking to them in their own language – where better to do that than in their networking meeting.

I spoke to an accountant who specialises in Law Firms and he regularly went to the networking events with lawyers – even though he was not, himself, a lawyer.

> *We had a Legal Firm as a client who were struggling to get leads. Their speciality was immigration law and work permits.*
>
> *Through a discussion with us we got them to find out conferences of techies, because we import a lot of technical expertise from overseas, they are often in need of work permits!*
>
> *Don't knock it – it worked!*

19. Sponsor a Meetup Group

This can prove to be an incredible way to get more sales, sponsor a Meetup Group where your prospects are likely to meet. Provide the food or the venue or some other form of sponsorship.

We have a small whitepaper guideline on Meetup Group sponsorships that is a must read before you do this. By sponsoring the Meetup Group you tell your prospective clients that you care about them and their professional network.

You can also use the networking events as a method to educate your prospects about either your product or if you really want to make a mark, educate them to solve a problem they are having.

20. Run your own Meetup

It is better to sponsor a mature Meetup Group in my opinion, than try and run your own, the time involvement is less and the profile you get will be higher – you will place yourself on the giving side of the equation....

Running your own networking group though is good if you can dedicate time to getting people there. I found a tax consultant doing this very well some years ago; he got Accountants to network (admittedly in small numbers) with the over-arching headline of tax training. It was a brilliant success for his tax consultancy.

Running a Meetup can be excellent for raising your profile if it works, it can be a disaster (and a costly one) if it fails.

If you do choose to run your own Meetup then don't run it on the cheap, use good quality catering and venue as this will reflect on your brand.

21. Open a Tab at the Local Bar

This worked for one client some years back. He wanted to get to know the people living in the plush but unsociable world of docklands and so he dropped a flyer round a couple of the apartment blocks saying he was having an event with a free bar.

His lead value was quite high and so if just a single person signed up he was likely to get his money back with a significant amount of profit.

You could do something a little bit less expensive like a wine tasting in the lobby or sponsor a school coffee morning or event. (See below under miscellaneous for some more about this idea)

22. Local Letts and Barter Networks

This can be a great source of soft referrals and if you are looking for affiliates amazing! These organisations are very local and very inward looking in many respects and as a local business (use the local business tag even if you are aiming to be an international conglomerate – after all Tesco's gets away with it...) you will get preference within the group.

Using barter networks can also be a great source of resources if you are running on a shoestring and as these organisations tend to be very ecological or green they can also increase your green profile.

23. Business Biscotti, Link4Coffee and Link4Growth

Mostly for those around London and the Home Counties – Business biscotti is a great way to meet new businesses, it has one downfall which is also its greatest strength for many who attend – it is very informal.

Remember informality can be a hindrance to doing good business; however, it is a great place to go to get your networking feet wet...

In addition, if you are networking at one or two of the more formal networking groups and one of your target audience goes then hey – what a great way to get meeting two.

24. The Elevator Pitch

Richard White has an excellent video on YouTube about creating the perfect elevator pitch. There are three basic sections to the perfect elevator pitch.

The First twenty seconds ae the most important, they need to grab your audience's attention and focus them into your message with an emotional appeal – how do your clients feel when they have the problem you solve, what motivates them to buy.

Then develop the theme, how do you help overcome that emotional pain, what is it you can solve for them?

Finally tell a short story that illustrates the problem fixed or the benefit of the fixed problem and the emotional payback!

25. 1 to 1s with local businesses

This is not a repeat! Actually go out of your way to knock on a few doors and introduce yourself, no need to sell, you could just use the phrase, hi there this is Bill, I just started a business locally and I wanted to pop over and say hi!"

We moved into a business centre a few years ago and one of the first things we did was to leaflet the rest of the businesses and then pop in to say hello – at least three businesses used us within a couple of months.

One of the keys to this was popping in to say hello, we just moved in….

This is cold calling, a friend of mine Michael Nicholaou runs Endex Pest Control a small pest control firm in East London. He has had incredible success visiting businesses and getting introductions to the business owner.

Angelika, From The Marketing Distribution Agency has had similar success with her distribution business. Door to door sales does not enjoy the profile it once had, but it does still work.

26. Customer Referrals

It amazes me how many small businesses do not ask for referrals from their customers. If you have done a good job you can just ask - "Hello Mel, we just finished printing your business cards, did you like them? Great – who do you know who needs new business cards, would you mind introducing me to them"

Then Follow up.

Then Say Thank you

Repeat.

Some people will speak of a referral strategy and this is very useful in your networking though not so much for client referrals.

Your referral strategy is a formal methodology that you use to educate those around you about what you do and what makes a good referral and how to spot it. If you are meeting with a group every week, think of taking one week in the month and dedicate it to "how to spot a lead for me"

27. Seminars and Training

This can be twinned with Video and webinars below as it requires the same resources and doing one means you can feed the other with material.

Training like The Sales Engine – Lead Generation Masterclass – places you as the pre-eminent authority on your subject, so running a couple of seminars and training session on a monthly basis will help you raise your profile and bring more leads.

It is also a great way of meeting new people.

> *I saw a great sales funnel for this. The company invited people on a low cost (donation ware) seminar ran in the evening during a quiet period.*

The attendees donated £10 to a nominated charity and then attended a 90-minute seminar on "writing copy" where they were given some really good advice.

At the end of the seminar (actually most of the way through it) they were offered the chance of signing up to a 1-day basic writing skills course.

This had a 30% conversion rate – in other words of the 20 people in the room 6 signed up.

These people and the others who attended were then offered a boot-camp advanced writing course which had a 20% conversion rate overall.

They were then offered an on-going coaching 12 months at a £50 a month which allowed them to submit 2 bits of writing to be critiqued 5% signed up.

Seminars and training can be a powerful tool.

The training company that did this enjoyed a massive return on their investment because of their donation ware experiment and they raised about £200 for charity.

Section 4 – Website Strategies

This can be seen as something of a dark art, many people see the website as the cure-all of their marketing strategy the magic potion, that if they get it right, it will solve all their sales woes.

And whilst for many people a website that is no more than a business brochure writ online is enough to ensure they don't embarrass themselves with a business card – however...

Depending on what you are selling your website can be one of the most powerful tools at your disposal. Most websites are pretty static, with little real-time interaction – you can quickly get an edge with yours if you can provide your visitor with exactly what they are looking for as they arrive.

When a client lands on your website there are a couple of things that they are expecting to see when they get there.

1) The answer to their question – What they typed in google.
2) Professional look at feel – not necessarily corporate expensive but clean – no placeholder text and try and avoid stock images if you can.
3) If you are selling products, show the products
4) Make the purchasing process easy, and upsell... even if you are selling services.

28. The Paradox of Choice

A quick word on active websites – a little is often enough, the same rule applies online as off-line – a single clear message – no mixing not confusion.

There is a well-known psychological principle called the Paradox of Choice which highlights that the more choices you give someone, the less happy they are with the choice that they make.

Websites that are clear and have a single defined purpose which is easy for the visitor to see.

29. Tracking Codes

It is so important to understand who is visiting your website and how they get there that I am going to say at the outset that a site that does not track visitor interactions and visitor spend is not worth having – even if it looks beautiful.

Using something like the X2Identity on X2CRM is perhaps one of the best ways to monitor interactions with clients and your website.

Tracking codes and analytics are complex and although we will mention a few ideas here, if you are not a web designer or coding expert, I would definitely get someone to add the code for you.

With google analytics, google will give you an overview of visitor behaviour when they come to your website. Although it is not perfect, it is a good way to spot trends and increases in traffic.

[Mouse Flow](#) is an incredibly powerful tool for watching what visitors do while they are on your website. It includes "mouse-tracking" to see where the customers point – and a heat map of where the most activity happens.

When someone is looking at your site from a laptop or desktop machine they will often move their mouse and eyes together – so where the mouse pointer is – is where they are looking.

If you have a powerful image on your site but it is taking the attention away from your call to action, then you will reduce conversions and sales…

Whoson (www.whoson.com) Let's you know "who" is browsing your site, using IP lookup and databases with registered IP addresses you can tell who is looking at your site – when they return and what they look at.

It also gives you a great pop-up chat tool with fantastic tracking that gives you great dynamic information well worth the $20-$45 a month price tag.

OpenTracker (www.opentracker.net) Is a similar product to Whoson, but with the advantage of giving you additional intelligence about your visitors and allow you to talk to the visitor in real time.

When you see where your visitors click, what pages they visit, this allows you to customise your sales message to convert as many visitors as possible to leads and sales.

In addition to this OpenTracker can also give you additional information on the companies that are visiting your website. They do this by using the public IP address database, which compared the Internet Address of the browser to a public record. It's not universally accurate, especially if the visitor is using a library or university internet connection, but it can bring some gems.

30. Online Chat

Using a tool like bold-chat or Clickdesk, greet your visitors when they come to your site and interact with them. Although it is better to have someone operating the chat line all the time, much can be gained even with a part time coverage.

If you are only going to cover the chat part time, it's better to let people know when to expect someone and try, as much as you can, to be there. So if you are only going operate the chat Monday and Tuesday Morning between 8am and 1pm – Make sure that is clear on the site.

When a visitor turns up on your site, set a small delay, let them get comfortable and then pop up a chat box and ask them if you can help. Make sure they have enough time to see what the site is all about before you bother them.

Chat boxes that do not disturb the browser are mixed blessings, they allow the visitor to continue browsing but they can also be ignored.

Some chat software allows you to see which page of your site your visitor is on, this helps you phrase your question accordingly.

31. Copy write your website

Although many of the people that land on your website are only going to be there for a few seconds, the serious will be looking for an excuse to buy from you. They have an itch, they are actively looking for someone who can scratch it, and poor copy will get them hitting the back button.

Amazingly, so few websites do this. Your site must make sense to people when they arrive, whilst getting the SEO guy to write your website is great for the rankings, it's not the best idea if you actually want people to read it!

Three important things to remember with copywriting.

1. Make the headline match the page purpose – answer the question that the visitor searched for.
2. Make sure the picture(s) match the article or page content, stock images are great but real images are better.
3. Use active voice as much as you can, "we wrote our whitepaper to help you write the perfect copy" talk to your visitor and – get straight to the point.
4. Avoid "double talk" – clean, clear and concise material gets people to a place of decision quicker than the

normal marketing gobbledegook.

32. Gather Email Addresses

Find a way to harvest email addresses by offering something of value to those visiting your website.

By the way, the word spam reduces sign-ups by 30% even if it is in the phrase "we will never spam you" – so don't say it! But don't spam people either.

Do not pop up your sign up box as soon as people land on your website – it's annoying. Give them a chance to read the content first. They don't know if it is worth signing up yet!

If you do use a pop over sign up box, make sure it is clear what the visitor is signing up for and make sure the pop-up is graphically pleasing. People will only sign up if they trust you.

33. Content, content, content

Are you looking for a good way to increase your search engine ranking? To establish yourself as an authority in your industry? To have a professional-looking webpage? Every webpage needs at least a little bit of content—but a lot of content is better.

Page content is integral to the success of a webpage (how else will anyone know what you're selling, if you don't tell them?), no matter what you sell.

Page content should be keyword-rich and search engine optimized so that your customers can find you. Having great, clean, original content is just as important for SEO as it is for sales.

One mistake many make is to put up poor quality content taken from someone else's website, if someone actually does get to your page, they will just hit the back button if the content is not clear and relevant.

When structuring page content, make sure that the point comes across as quickly as possible. Be clear and consistent and use a tone that will appeal to your customer.

34. Change

Search engines like Google and MSN prefer websites that have fresh content and vastly prefer websites that have content that is actually relevant to the keywords inside the content and to the purpose of the website. This means that updating your website is key to improving your search engine ranking.

Content, like the webpage itself, will become stale over time. Repeat customers will stop coming back to the website if they feel that it is not being taken care of, not unlike with a bricks and mortar shop. Think of your website like a physical office or store—it occasionally needs to be dusted, vacuumed, or even completely redecorated to ensure it is presentable to clients or customers.

Change is a good thing. Tweak your content to ensure that it reflects the most current information and that it is fresh and lively. If there is any content that is not relevant to the purpose of the website—remove it. It can get your website flagged and downgraded in search results.

While you should not make changes just for the sake of making changes, do ensure that you make updates that improve your website's relevancy and makes it more reader friendly.

35. Target pages

Each page on your website should have a single job. Don't use a single page as your contact page and to tell the story of your business. Not only can this make information difficult to find, it can also lead to an overstuffed, confusing website. One page should have one purpose and one very clear call to action.

Using target pages can bring your Google AdWords cost per click down and improve your conversions from web traffic. If someone searches for "Lambeth Accountant" and finds a page which says "Lambeth's best Accountant" do you think they might be interested?

Laziness is an enemy here, don't scrimp on pages – you don't have to stick them all in the menu, in fact quite the opposite – let them have the menu so people can explore but leave them off the menu if there are too many of them.

A user comes to your webpage looking for something specific. The faster they can find it, the more likely they are to respond to your call to action. The more difficult it is to find, the more likely they are to hit the back button and do business with someone else.

Don't confuse your page visitors—target your pages precisely to the search terms they used to get there.

36. Call to action

Every page should include a clear call to action.

- Click here to save money now.
- Call this number and get a free quote
- Buy now and save 40%
- Add to basket
- Request a free no-risk call back
- Talk to Us – button
- Let's do it – I particularly like this one as it works nicely on the end of a long sales page.

The call to action should be clear and concise but also include the reason if it can.

37. Squint Test

I freely admit to stealing this one, but for the life of me I cannot remember where from. The call to action on your website should be the clearest item on the page.

Take a look at your landing page and then squint at it – is your call to action the clearest part of the page, if not then redesign the page so that it is.

38. Call back button

A call back button allows people who visit your site to click a button and get a call back from you.

This will greatly increase the number of enquiries you get from your website, it reduces the clients perceived risk and gives you a chance to prove your efficiency. This is incredibly powerful for support type industries like Computer Engineers.

Also a call back button tells a visitor that you are serious about communication and in the service industry that is very important.

39. Long Sales Page / Landing Page

Writing landing pages is an art that you can learn easily, using long but structured copy that sells on multiple levels.

With a long copy page, you start with enough information for a fast decision and enough interest for a slow decision, as the reader moves down the page they get more and more reasons to buy and more and more benefits – emotional and practical benefits.

It is OK to include a feature list but do not make features the point of sale.

Provide your call to action so that it appears wherever the browser is on the page. Either include several versions of the button (each one unique) or get one of those nice whizzy buttons that follows down the page.

40. Banner Exchanges

This works really well for the crafts industries where they have banner rings. These rings advertise each other's banner usually free in return for having other people's banners on your site.

Buy banner advertising, if it can be targeted, niched to the people you want to speak to – then it's worth it.

Adverts telling you that you will be seen on 100,000 websites are to be avoided as too broad.

Also Google Banner Ads – we are going to do a special section on SEM (search Engine Marketing) but once again be careful – it can be expensive if done wrong.

41. Link Exchanges

Anywhere that links to you is good, especially if it is ranked high in google (not necessarily no 1 in Google, see page ranking in SEM section) – Link farming is frowned upon by google but it can be effective in helping promote your website.

The important thing with Link exchanges and "backlinks" in general is that they are on pages which are relevant to what you do. If you are selling clothes a link from an IT website is not really going to help you very much.

42. Blogging

Blogging is a great way of providing content to your website. Keyword rich blogs can really have an impact on your conversions and on the type of visitors that visit your website.

Firstly, I would have the blog attached to your website but also update those blogs to social media platforms when you think they are powerful enough (try one a month or one every couple of weeks)

Keep the blog to a single keyword group, i.e. "Lambeth Accountant", or "Impact of Inheritance tax on Basic Rate taxation". Rather than trying to cover everything, you do, be specific about a particular product or better still a particular problem.

If you sell health food supplements an article on how health food supplements work is not as good as an article on Homeopathic remedies for high blood pressure.

Provide links to your own content but also link to others content and articles as it encourages people to return to your site or blog for more information on an ongoing basis.

Also, this is a great opportunity for you to get people to sign up to get updates to your blog in their email, harvesting email addresses to feed into your nurture campaigns.

43. Guest Blogging

Do you know someone who you want to blog on your site? How about a supplier, a partner even a client! Well cross guest blogging with links is going to help your site getting noticed.

What works well is that you provide each other content and then links between one site/blog and the other. This gives you both google fodder and provides your readers and followers with even more useful content.

To get guest bloggers, I would approach people with a plan, a pre-written piece and a firm proposal about how this will happen.

Just as an aside, re-use content of course but rewrite the articles so that the search engines recognise them as different pages. Some search engines hate repeat articles and may well penalise you for it.

44. Webinars

Schedule regular webinars to showcase your products or services, The sales engine 'writing good copy' and 'sales CRM' webinars are good examples of what we mean. Allow people to interact with you and ask questions.

Provide a mixture of freemium and paid for content. Of course nothing is free, when the client registers for the webinar, ask for their name and email address and telephone number.

45. Videos

Videos are powerful at the moment, make videos about your products, about your services, about the events you run and the people in your office, post them online and promote them. Video everything and post it with good keyword and content to YouTube.

Go further if you can and get your clients to give you video testimonials and put them on your site, nothing says success better than a client being willing to go on record and tell people how good you are.

Target your ads to the video you just posted and your leads will click through to you!

63% of the population are visual learners, why are we always trying to tempt them with words….

Section 5 - Real Media

Real media has gone a bit out of fashion, I suspect because people see social media and digital assets as a cheaper way to be noticed.

But research suggests that getting a personalised and relevant communication through your door or as a hand-out in the street is still a very powerful way to attract clients.

The typical response rate for a door dropped flyer is between 0.5% and 1%, so for every thousand flyers you distribute you are looking at between 5 and 10 enquiries. This is dependent on a lot of things including the quality of the material, the clearness of the message and the call to action and the desirability of what you are offering.

Some leaflets can get a massive 10% response rate if they hit the right spot and have the best call to action.

46. Designing Stunning Media

It can cost a fortune to design things using a professional designer but there are some really good shortcuts. We found Canva.com to be an incredible resource – so much so we paid to go pro!

Canva allows you to drag and drop design elements onto your page and then export the result in a print ready format.

www.canva.com

I am sure there are others but we have found this to be the best of breed!

One of the really useful features of Canva is their design academy, really useful for getting free design help and making sure your media looks professional.

47. Sponsor a school or club

Sponsor something like the PTA (excellent for coffee shops – sponsor the PTA by allowing them to use a room at the coffee shop for free – provide water and a couple of jugs of coffee the first couple of times) get a mention in the newsletter and of course footfall.

Sponsor the school mag, or the club newsletter – it will cost about £50 but will give you a great – local, focused group. I know a school clothing outlet that gets all their business from this method.

Great for photographers or anyone who trades with families.

48. Parish Magazines

They seem to have gone out of fashion but if you are a member of a church or religious organisation and there is a magazine, see if your business can sponsor it – usually it is inexpensive, you are the only advert in it and the readers are happy – especially if they know you.

I know of a plumber in Worcester who gets about half his business as referrals from his local church community. His advert in the Local Church magazine once a quarter is enough to remind the other 30 or so members of the church what he does and to look out for work for him.

49. Publish a local newsletter or magazine

I saw an estate agent do this locally in east London and it was quite effective, they did of course advertise their own properties in the newsletter but they also made sure it was relevant to the local community and it achieved a wide readership. This can take a little bit of work but if you have a budding reporter in your midst, it need not be hard.

BTW – Paper not app! You can do an app but it's much more effective if you produce paper.

It can take a while for a paper like this to get established, especially if you are aiming at a certain catchment of people. Be prepared for a long haul to get the magazine to where you want it....

50. Hawkers and fluffy suits

Ok so we have all seen the power of Ronald McDonald when he wanders around outside that famous store, how the kids are drawn to him like a magnet. Try your own version. A friend of mine is determined to find someone to dress up as a rat and give out his pest control flyers down the high street.

This idea works especially well if you sell things to families. Some firms will hire you the suit and someone to stand in it and do the leaflet drop for you. Aim at the high street and remember you may have to get permission.

You don't have to have a big fluffy suit of course, you can achieve something similar with helium balloons and sweets in the high street.

51. Flyers in doors

Leafleting is a very powerful medium as you can see in our introduction to this section. Leaflets that are well designed can delivery between 5 and 10 enquiries per 1,000 flyers dropped through letterboxes.

Remember though a few golden rules.

- Choose the Leaflet Company Carefully
- Make sure they delivery your leaflet intelligently – if you are a landscape gardener you don't want your leaflets dropped into council tower blocks!
- If possible, check the delivery yourself.
- Use a tracking telephone number so you can measure response.

- Use a tracking website to track response.
- Make sure there is a good reason to respond – a compelling call to action (discounts, time limits, scarcity, deadlines – all help)
- Don't hold back on leaflet quality – a good quality leaflet speaks volumes to the client about what quality of service they are going to receive.

Dropping flyers through doors can be surprisingly cost effective and if you can do something about targeting the flyers in precise areas then you can get a massive increase in the effectiveness of your campaign.

It costs about £150 to print 10,000 flyers or postcards. It also costs about £550 to have them distributed – your total cost for a flyer campaign is about £700 equivalent of 7p for leaflet.

If you get 50 responses they cost you £14 each enquiry and if you close half of those (25) then the cost per sales is £28. Usually you will get closer to 75 calls (reducing the cost per sale to about £20).

However, we want to drill a little deeper than that, if your clients stay with you for a long period then you should be working on the lifetime value of the client.

52. Car drop

This actually works quite well if you have an auto business, find where cars are parked and put a flyer under the wiper blade. Just be careful where you do this as some car-park owners will object.

To get a better return on your campaign, try just targeting certain cars….

I.e. if you are valeting cars, perhaps just put the flyer under the wiper blades on dirty cars…. Or clean cars… Clean cars are people you know like having clean cars and are more likely to use your car cleaning service – dirty car owners – do they care? If your offering strong enough to bring them across to idea of a clean car?

53. Coffee Shop and Supermarket Noticeboards

This one can be quite powerful if you are intending to reach "mums", especially stay at home mums, as they are most likely the ones browsing these boards.

Works especially well for things like network selling (pyramid selling schemes), fitness and alternative health.

54. Table Stickers

This is a great idea if you can do it – fantastic for the yummy mummy catchment…

Ask the local quality coffee shop if they will allow you to put a transfer advert on their table tops – they will probably charge you a little for this but the results can be amazing.

This technique takes your marketing to where your customers congregate. By being on the table of the coffee shop, you are guaranteed the type of people who read your advert and so you know exactly how to word your advert or offer.

I haven't tried this yet but I bet if you offered to pay for the patrons Wi-Fi access you could get stickers on the table pretty easily.

55. Project an image

This can be very powerful if you have a shop, put a video projector aimed to the pavement outside your shop. This will allow you to project an image onto the pavement – it's an attractor!

If you have the budget get some animated videos with speech bubbles or even a couple of speakers.

What is cool about this is that it will attract buyers after your shop closes and you will be remembered.

If you do this right and change the images or cartoons on a regular basis, you stand a good chance of becoming a landmark – wouldn't it be nice if everyone met outside your shop.

56. Sky Light Campaign

How about projecting your own bat logo onto the clouds – it worked for batman and it could work for you. Lasers a great for pinpointing where you are – though you do need to get planning permission for using them.

57. Blimp!

Not for everyone but ideal if you are in the middle of an industrial estate, get a blimp and let it float above your store – there is a guy who sells tyres just off the A406 in East London, it's great you know exactly where he is.

58. A Sandwich Board

This can be quite effective if used right. Someone stands on the street with an ad board front and back and a bundle of flyers. Great if your store is hidden in a back street behind the high street. I think the costume is the best idea but it's not for everyone…

Using this method, your advert can move around, hand out flyers and if you train them right, they can answer questions – at least where you are.

59. Feather and Banner

There is much to be said on this subject, I have yet to find anyone who it won't work for. A feather banner has a simple weighted base and wand like vertical pole – from this pole hangs a banner – it's quite effective as it looks cool and can have a single simple message on it – "Here I AM"

These feather banners are inexpensive, made from lightweight materials that are easy to carry and can be very eye-catching, especially in the wind!

60. Shopping Centre Concession

Get permission from the local massive shopping centre to set up a simple 1 man stand, hand out flyers and brochures and talk to people. Once again this depends on what you are selling but it does quite well for the right products – this can be done with stations and larger shops.

If you are a lawyer or Accountant – you can do this at the weekend and man it with a marketing team who are trained to take notes and pass on the information for you to close the deals with the clients on Monday.

61. Local Shops – Business Cards

This is great if you have a business that's aimed at a particular small community, I know a Portuguese electrician who has his cards in just two Portuguese restaurants and that with word of mouth is all he needs to keep his books filled.

Another creative locksmith I know uses the local static Cobblers who also cuts keys to give out his business cards – this accounts for a large percentage of his new business sales as the clients come looking for new keys but often ask about a locksmith.

62. Posters/Infographic

This is more about being able to display your idea as a picture, especially if what you sell has a degree of complexity about it.

Let's say you run a company specialising in security systems for peoples' homes. You could do an infographic pointing out common security problems with people's homes and what you can do to resolve those problems.

An infographic is a visual way of displaying complex graphic data so that people can understand it at a glance.

These also make great sales tools, something you can hand out to your salesforce to carry with them to clients – they can leave them behind for the client to look at when they have gone.

63. Postcard Campaign

A funny postcard addressed directly to the householder, or business holder will get a lot of attention, if you have a brilliant joke or cartoon, it's possible that they will put the postcard somewhere prominent so they can see it – if it is "on target" they will see it when you need it.

We did a joke postcard 7 years ago in the IT business and I still see it on people's desk from time to time when I go and visit them.

Something funny or cute is likely to hang around more than a serious message and if it appeals to the clients' sense of the absurd, it is likely to last a while on their desk.

64. BookMark HowTo

Design a bookmark, something that is inexpensive and useful but also has some very useful information on it.

We designed a bookmark we gave out for free entitled - 6 Tips for YouTube success – we only actually put 5 items on the bookmark the 6th item was available from a YouTube video accessed via our website and a sign-up form.

65. Direct Mail

Direct mail is increasingly effective as people move away from it. People actually get a lot less junkmail through the door than they used to and well-presented direct mail can have an incredible effect for you.

The typical response rate for Direct mail campaigns is 4.4%, if you consider the costs involved can be a very effective use of marketing budget.

If you deliver 1,000 personally addressed letters to an area and you do a reasonable job (same rules as apply everywhere else for marketing) then you will get about 44 enquiries. If you assume that the campaign has cost you £500 in postage and printing you are looking at a lead cost rate of just £11.36.

By the way, if you are direct mailing streets of people in a particular area – dispense with the post office and get a distribution company aboard – it's cheaper.

Target your audience well, don't waste money on numbers try and get to specific people or market groups.

Be creative. One idea we used a couple of years ago for the support business was a bit of a risk but it worked.

We bought a couple of hundred lilac envelopes, and note size sheets of paper and we printed a handwritten message, addressed the envelopes in fountain pen, "by Hand" and dropped it through the doors of a well-known well to do area.

We took 6 jobs from a single street – not bad for £50 and £15 to a daughter to deliver.

Section 6 – Phone Campaigns

Telephone campaigns can be quite scary to start, but get a few calls under your belt and you will soon be calling like a pro. If you are nervous, try doing the internal campaigns first.

66. Telemarketing

Telemarketing gets a lot of bad press, yes it's annoying, yes it is hard work, yes it takes someone tough to do it – but it works. It's not a pure numbers games and the hints and tips below will help you get the most out of the telesales campaign.

The best people to call are those who already know you, for example the people you meet networking. If you call them straight after you meet them, they are more likely to take your call, remember who you are and spend some time speaking to you.

Telemarketing has the highest response rate of all the direct marketing methods, it's a whopping 6.16% for businesses and 10.16% for homes.

67. Sell or Don't Sell

If you are telemarketing, either sell or don't sell. Go into the call knowing what it is you want out of it and be sure to have your script reflect that. A great way of not selling is by surveying your lead base for information that you can later use to market your services.

"hello <Firstname> I am Yash from ABC consultants, you met my principle Mark a few months ago and he has asked me to give you a call to see if you would mind answering a few survey questions for him?"

68. Cross Selling and Upselling

The cheapest leads are those who have already bought from you. They trust you and they will nearly always take your call.

We used this to great effect with the IT business, we called clients who had just bought Anti-Virus from us and asked them about their backup. About 20% upgraded over the course of the campaign (5 days) doubling the revenue from those clients.

Use this in conjunction with an upgrading/cross selling email campaign and you will have an amazingly powerful tool.

It costs very little to sell to an existing client…

69. Affiliate Marketing

This can be done via the phone and once again when coupled with another campaign type can produce quite amazing results. If you sell utilities to clients (Gas, electric etc.) try selling someone else's stuff to the same client base for an affiliate commission.

Remember a client who has already bought from you is likely to buy from you again. However, you should not be on the phone to them every week like Del Boy with yet another bargain to tempt them with.

Affiliate marketing though is a good idea; a couple of affiliate campaigns a year (maximum 3 or 4) will make a big difference to your income.

70. Refine the List

The First stage of telemarketing or a telesales campaign is to refine the list of people you are going to call, make sure that they meet the criteria of the people who are likely to need your services.

Remove from the list, people who hate you, people who can't afford you, people who do something like what you do and finally people who have never interacted with you. This will leave you with about 20% of your contacts – good, this is your hotlist.

71. Write a script

I hate reading scripts but there is something powerful about knowing what you are going to say in advance of answering the phone, a sense of focus and direction.

The script does not need to be word for word, it can be just headlines and direction – especially if you are going to be doing it yourself or if you have a garrulous marketer who can get on with people.

Try to find a compelling reason for the prospect to continue to talk to you – it is all about them after all. Sometimes you can combine an account management call with an existing customer with an exploration to see if they need this new series.

Be clear about your outcome – An appointment or a sale or …

72. Record the Call

Audio recording is "ok" but what I mean here is keep a track of what calls you have made to the client, what you have spoken about and what you have agreed to do for them.

For example: - if the prospect says they are too busy then ask them when would be more convenient, then book it into your diary – when you call them back you can say "Hi John, it's Sharif, you asked me to give you a call in the new year to discuss your marketing needs"

Of course, this is great with gatekeepers "I have an appointment booked with John for a telephone conversation" will often get you straight through without a delay.

73. Can you answer a survey

A couple of years ago surveys were the thing for getting people engaged. It is still a powerful tool although most people will see through your thin façade if you are not careful…

An amazingly powerful tool is to survey your own clients. This can provide you brilliant material for refining your product or service.

"Hello John, I wonder if you have a couple of minutes to help me out. What would you say our greatest strength is as a business? Thank you and our biggest weakness? Really, I will look into that and see if we can improve that. "

Client surveys can also reveal buying needs, "I wish you did …." I once picked up a 12k sale from this line!

74. Test and measure!

This will repeat several times through this document, don't do anything without it. Test and measure your responses to the calls you make, if your opening gambit does not get a good response try a different one – keep changing until you find something that engages the other person.

One great story I heard was about a web developer who started a campaign by calling his prospect list and telling them their website was down! He got 100% of their attention...

Section 7 – Other Ideas

There are lots of other ideas that you can use and adapt to your own needs.

If you have something have not listed here – email me.

sharif@howdoigetmoresales.com

75. Partnerships

This is perhaps one of the most overlooked tools in your tool chest. Make partnerships; create win-win alliances to help bring in more business.

At Cloudberry, we had a strategic alliance with 3 ISPs, we were there onsite support people for a certain type of customer. If they needed to do more than just send a router they passed the client onto us. We spent a total of about 20 hours on each partnership and the rewards were incredible. They were by far the biggest source of customers for us.

This is the most important thing that you will do.

Sit down and think about people who could – potentially – use your service. I will use the example here of a Property Lawyer.

She wants to speak to people who are moving home, she now that when people move home they discuss it with: -

1) Estate agents
2) Mortgage Brokers (IFAs)
3) Business Transfer Agents.

She would go out of her way to meet these people and to cultivate them into business partners. If I were advising her – she would be holding a monthly free event for estate agents involving alcohol and food. She would be taking the bosses out for dinner and offering to put the Lawyer in their office free of charge for half a day a month.

76. Distribution – Products and Services

Distribution channels are great for getting your product to a wider audience. Generally, you would use distribution if selling a physical product but there is no reason why you can't do it if you are selling a service.

For example, if you run a beauty salon, try selling your experience packs through retail outlets. Till-side upgrades….

If you do holistic therapies, try marketing them through the beauty therapists.

The secret of distribution is in fact margin. Can the distribution channel make a good return on the product?

Sale or return really helps here, reducing the risk to the distribution outlet. This is easier if you are selling a service.

77. Brochure

Create a brochure, in printed and PDF form, to give to prospects, it makes you look better, which is good but it also saves a lot of work on the quote stage.

Brochures should be A4 and well printed, don't do it on the LaserJet at home!!

They should be either folded A3 or Bound A4 in size and should have about 15% coverage of words vs graphics on average.

Keep the paragraphs short, keep a minimum number of paragraphs to headings and no more than 3 headings and a title per page side.

BTW, I don't put pricing on marketing material except if you have a products page on the website.

78. Productise your service

Often it is very hard for people to make a decision to buy from you because they are not sure either what they need or what it is going to cost. One of the best ways to overcome this is to productise a service offering.

For example: - If you offer IT support, you could offer a set monthly package for remote helpdesk support for a fixed fee.

We at the Sales Engine offer a social media package which includes whitepaper, blogs, emails and twitter feeds for a simple price of £100 per month.

79. Make a Banner

This works especially well for events or if you have a wall or fence outside your building. Even better if you can get someone else to host it for you.

- Must be clear and easy to read

- Big enough to be read by passing traffic (car or foot)
- Compelling language
    - Be Healed today!
    - Boot Fayre here!
- Date and Time clearly visible
- Single Message

80. Hand out Free...

This is a surprisingly good secondary tactic. I suggest something you can get inexpensively but there are a couple of things that really work well.

Pens are good and are kept for a long time (until they run out) and good quality pens can sometimes last years. I just signed a contract with a client who used the pen I gave them about 5 years ago. It has my company name and my telephone number on it. But – beware, this is not necessarily going to produce leads. When did you last buy from the side of a pen?

Fridge magnets are good if they are cute or funny, if not they won't be used.

Water is good – Don't look at me like that! Water is a brilliant give away – Costco were doing mineral water last month for 36 bottles for 3.60 +VAT if I remember correctly the cost of the give-away – 10p!!

Re-wrap the bottle with your own label (don't forget to include the ingredients stuff) and add your own marketing. I would not advise using "branded" water – too expensive and too much risk of them getting antsy if it works.

Free food and drink always goes well but beware, once it's gone so has your message.

Section 8 - Exhibitions

81. Small Exhibitions

The London Means Business Exhibition taught me a lot about exhibiting my business and I think they are well worth attending. Find small business expo's and set up a stand for the day. It is important to do several things in an exhibition and they are nearly all listed already – I am going to repeat some stuff here as it works slightly differently with an expo.

The advantage of small exhibitions is that they are much more flexible than the larger operators are, the space is not usually so strict, things like power and internet are usually provided free of charge.

The disadvantage is the footfall; it can be variable. I would suggest using a cost per lead calculation of something like £1.20 per signed up visitor – that makes it about £2.40 per actual visitor and about £4.80 per "suspect/lead"

So if the event is expecting 100 people, there will be about 50 attendees about half of whom would be leads. The maximum to spend on the exhibition space would be £120.00

You should ask a couple of questions before you commit to the show: -

1) How many visitors did you have in this particular show last time?
2) Can I have the visitor list (add 50p per registered visitor to your budget if the answer is yes)
3) How many exhibitors are exhibiting for a second time?
4) Call references and ask them how they did – be specific
    a. Did you get any sales?
    b. How many leads did you get?

c. How was the event organisation?

These events are rarely cheap so be sure to give yourself a better than even chance of winning.

Also the advertised rate is usually nowhere near the price you can get the stand for if you haggle. I would estimate that most entry level packages can be had for about 25% or more off.

82. Purpose

Why are you doing this, what is the purpose of the stand? If you are aiming for sales, how are you going to achieve them on the stand? Are you aiming for appointments – why should people book an appointment with you?

If you want to get quote appointments, book them on the day and confirm them by email (and of course turn up on time)

If you are just looking to raise awareness – I hope your pocket is big!

> *As I am writing this book, I have just got back from the Technology for Marketing and Advertising exhibition at Olympia in London. It was a great show with a lot of top quality products on display.*
>
> *One problem though, although I was dressed smartly, showed intelligent interest and classic buying signs – no one tried to close me!*
>
> *5 day later I got bombarded with dispassionate spam emails thanking me "personally" for attending the stand.*

You are there to make a sale! So....

83. Preparation

Preparing for an exhibition is key to success or failure. There are several things you can do to improve the success of the exhibition, most of which are inexpensive.

1) Email all your prospects and invite them to the expo.
2) Book appointments on the stand with people
3) Offer a free "clinic" to help people with their issues relating to what you do.
4) Email your clients and invite them to visit, then introduce them to your prospects (this works really well – a live un looked for testimonial)
5) Printing – done in advance
6) Set a mini marketing plan.

Remember the real cost of an exhibition is not just the hall hire; it is also the cost of time on the stand and the cost of follow up.

84. Email Campaign

Send a small email campaign to get people from your prospects and clients to come and visit you at the exhibition, be sure to keep track of who visits and of course email them a thank you for visiting the stand.

Extend this campaign to after the event for about 60 days. Build the campaign on the same theme as the stand; this lends more power to the messages of your campaign and to the stand itself if you re-use it in another event.

As an example, if you use the exhibition to launch a new product or service (one of the main reasons for doing an exhibition) then your email campaign will build upon that launch.

The email campaign could follow the following track:-

1) Come and see us at – Customers and Leads
    a. Email and telephone campaign as well if you have time.

b. Also send a direct mail (paper) invite to those people most likely to attend – you will get a better response if you use multiple channels.
c. Twitter and Facebook – events and posts to support the event as well.
d. Also, consider doing a series of Blogs on LinkedIn and your site to promote your attendance.

2) New Product Launch – Send this email to Customers and leads to tantalise your audience and encourage them to attend.

Remember; when someone visits your stand that you invited that means they are interested in you and/or your product.

3) See you tomorrow – Send this email to customers and leads who have said that they will come to the event.
   a. Also send a "wish you were here" to the others who did not respond and maybe offer them something to encourage attendance.
   b. What a great show – if the show is more than one day – queue this to go off towards the end of day 1.
4) Thanks for Visiting us – Send a Thank You to everyone who visited your stand and include an "extension" of your stand offer. This is a great way to remind the people who visited your stand about what you do and what you offered on the day.

a. The last event I went to was a marketing event held at London's Olympia. I was quite excited to see how things were done. Imagine my amazement when the only email I got the next day was from the event organiser thanking me for attending a seminar I couldn't find!
b. Hot Leads must be called within 24 hours of the event – imperative and keep calling until you get them – don't give up. If you don't contact a lead within 24 hours of the event, you reduce the potential to convert by at least 63%

c. Exclude hot leads from this email but include them on a follow up email that confirms anything you agreed at the event and warns them of your impending call.
5) Sorry we missed you – send this email to those who said they would come but didn't, you could send an email that says "sorry we missed you, hope everything is OK, let me know if you would like to hear more about our special offer at the event stand"
6) Freemium offer – to anyone who attended.

Then add these contacts to your general nurture campaigns if they have not activated a lead sequence.

With the right tools, all of this can happen automatically and with very little intervention from you or your sales team.

85. Banners

Your stand is very important at an exhibition it reflects on your business and your professionalism. My advice is, if you cannot afford a good stand; then do not buy a stand at all! Go for a table with a chair behind it and some posters tacked to the shell.

Pop-Up Banner stands are inexpensive but check three things before you buy.

1) The Thickness of Banner Material. Should be thick enough not to curl at the edges, 8 – 11mil is usually OK.
2) The Stand must have a heavy base and not tend to lean forwards (if yours does lean forward use a pencil under the front feet it works wonders.)
3) Print Quality – It is worth remembering that not all

printers are the same – some cannot handle solid colours very well and some do not colour match. Check first.

Freestanding curved stands are much better because they make you look much more professional they are also sturdier and provide a better backdrop.

Here are some other general banner guidelines

1) Try not print below the table top height (or do not print anything important below table to height) if you are exhibiting behind a table then no-one will see it.
2) Get Lights – floor level LEDs are effective as are high-level spots.
3) Keep your message simple – just one simple message that is clear and customer

centric. For example:- "Massively increase your sales from networking" is better than "we are the best networking group" because of the focus of the message.
4) Not too many words! IF you can get away with your company name and a picture of your product ending 120cm from the ground then you have a perfect banner!
5) Use large, clear lettering and don't let style overtake substance and clarity.
6) Include your Website and Telephone number so people can note them down. Use a special website for events that way you can track traffic that is a result of the event specifically.

7) There is no need to include your email address, twitter or any other extraneous details. No-one will pay attention to them and they clutter up your message.

86. Setting up a Stand

Setting up a stand can be fraught with difficulties if you have not done it before. There are some do's and don'ts as well as a few ideas to help you make the most of your space.

1) Make sure you know how much space you are getting and make sure your banner fits in it. Some Exhibitions are very strict about space – check first.
2) Power – Ask the question, can I have power to my stand – you need this for your lights, which as I said above are essential to make your stand – stand out.
3) Internet Access – If you need internet access make sure of it

before you book the stand and then test it the day before. Check also for 4G signal and have a standby, especially if you are demonstrating your product online.
4) Best Position for your stand – Most people turn left when they enter the exhibition space and you would imagine that the first stand on the left would get the most traffic – not so! The Stand opposite the entrance to the left will get the footfall – if it is big enough – if not the third and fourth positions facing the door to the left. My favourite place is near the toilets (preferably with the foot flow) – my advice would be to keep clear of refreshment areas entrances and exits on busy exhibitions as too crowded to be effective.
5) Sell something on the stand. If you sell a product, bring it with

you and a credit card machine and sell it there and then. People are there with their chequebooks and ready to spend!
6) Set Up your stand in the office before you go. This gives you a chance to see what it looks like without distraction, make sure you have everything you need (do a list – honestly it's best)
7) Remember the extension leads.
8) Set up the stand as early as you can the day before is good, especially if you have a complex stand or you have not set it up before. Test your presentations and your media as well as your screens and your staff.
9) Pack it all away by numbers. Create a list of what you need, when you set the stand up and then number everything and make sure it's packed away

and unpacked when you get to the other end.
10) Print materials professionally, remember that whatever people take away from your stand reflects on your branding and on your reputations. Exhibitions are all about giving people the impression that you are successful and can make them successful – look successful.
   a. Avoid photocopies and home printed brochures.
   b. Think about the brochure "finish" it's OK for it not to be glossy but it should be quality. I love using thicker paper and special finishes – it is so different from everyone else's materials it gets noticed.

11) Give-aways – Think about your give-aways carefully – Sweets (wrapped), Pens, Bags, USB Sticks, reports (blah), Mouse mats – how much do you want to spend! Sweets are essential though – water is better….

   a. When you give things away, think about how they will reflect on your business. As I am writing this I am looking at a pen that I picked up from an exhibition recently, it is a very cheap green biro, which never worked – The sort you can buy 20 for £1 from PoundLand. The company that was giving it away sell very expensive data!
   b. If you can, brand everything! When we have sweets on the stand, we choose them

by colour. Orange and Black sweets (they exist I promise).
   c. Try to have a mixture of things including some high value stuff that you can give to "genuine" enquiries.
12) All marketing material should give a good clear reason to visit your website and sign up. A promise of an item of value like a free report or eBook. The more reason you give your visitors and potential clients to stay in touch, the better your interactions will be.

87. Collect Information

Collect business cards, peoples contact details (use the zapper if they have one but collect them independently as well as the data sometimes takes too long to come through)

Collect as much relevant intelligence about the visitor as you can. Write the information on the card or an enquiry sheet and store the information efficiently. If your business relies on certain metrics then you should be collecting those metrics while speaking with people and storing them on your system.

If you run an IT company that only deals with Macs then it is important to know if the people you are speaking with are using Mac's – so ask and RECORD! You should make sure your CRM has the capability to record these metrics and act upon them when you need it.

When we did the Lambeth means business expo a couple of years ago, Andrew and I had a key we used on the cards of the people we collected.

BA – meant we gave them a free copy of Andrews Book

BS – A free copy of Sharif's Book

X – Meant call them straight back – live lead

XX – Meant a sale

Line through the card meant throw away.

Last Exhibition I did I took photos of the business cards and sent them offshore for entering on the database and tagging while we were still exhibiting. In one case, the prospect got the follow-up before we finished speaking!

Remember we are not looking to sell to everyone – be willing to let people go!

88. A Stand Dance

We have found that it is good to have a primary and secondary role on the stand, one-person stands and sells and another fields.

If I were talking to a client who was a real prospect, I would face them directly and talk to them face to face using what is called a closed stance. If I was in a closed stance and someone else approached me the secondary staff member would greet them and hold them while I was talking.

If the person I was talking to was not relevant to what we were looking for, I would open the conversation and even go as far as inviting the secondary into the conversation and then discretely move out of it.

If the Secondary member had a live lead and I was in open position, he knew he could interrupt and we would swap visitors.

This sounds quite complex but it did actually work, we were about 80% more effective using this method.

You may like to work out a process that makes sense to your stand team, but work out how you are going to make sure you have the right person talking to the right visitor. Find a way that you can communicate with each other without spooking the visitors.

89. Engagement Script

"Hello Sir, can I ask your name?"

"What do you do?"

"That's fascinating, so you must know all about …."

That was the basic idea behind most of our engagement scripts in the IT company, especially when we were looking for clients that needed to be compliant.

Actually an engagement script should ask relevant questions that pre-qualify a lead/visitor to your stand for a discussion about your product.

The secret is to ask a lot of questions until a conversation happens.

Not interrogation but questions about the visitor in order to find a place where you can build rapport in the context of your stand.

90. Hire Expo Staff

Never have an undermanned stand – if you don't have enough people to run the stand don't set up, it is better not to show than have a bad stand and not follow up on the leads you get.

Your stand staff should be well trained in the basics of your offering; they should know your elevator pitch and your basic engagement script.

Teach them the day before – pay for it if you need to and make sure they understand the dance that you have planned.

You want to make sure your stand is adequately staffed but on the other hand, you don't want too many spare bodies either. Our suggestion is to have at least one technical and two exhibition staff on a simple stand.

91. Working the Room

Many stand owners spend the whole day on the stand; this is not a good idea, work your way around the room to the other stands. Make sure you speak with all the other stand-owners – you have a couple of ice-breakers already.

"Hello have you been here before – how did it go?"

"Hello how's your day going so far?"

"Hello – do you want a free cupcake, sweet, book or mouse mat?"

My best business from exhibitions is nearly always from other stand holders.

As an aside, see if you can get everyone who is on the stand to work the room. This gives you a greater chance of "clicking" with the other stallholders. Also talk about their offerings so you have a few "Ahh

Sharif was just telling me about that" moments.

One networking stand at an event I attended went from stand to stand with a massive bottle of champagne giving all the stands a free glass of bubbly at the start and towards the end of the day. Do the same thing or maybe just hand out water (branded with your own brand) and you have a great way of the other stands remembering you.

92. Follow Up

Before you drop the stand for the night, get your data distributed, if you can afford to have someone entering the data live into your CRM then you have an advantage over all the other exhibitors, your thank you for visiting our stall can hit their mailbox before they even leave the venue.

We found that having forms we attached cards to worked for getting additional information but tended to be cumbersome – after much "jiggery and pokery" we found it was just easier to have a thin permanent marker and to code the cards AFTER the visitor left the stand.

One of the advantages of staffing an exhibition stand properly is that you have enough time to be sure you capture as many of your audience dynamics as you can; and you can record them in a way that can be referred to and used in future.

Mark out the visitors for immediate follow up and call them within 24 hours – after that you may as well throw the cards away and write off the event as a dead loss.

If you have booked appointments, get email confirmations out (use appointments in Outlook to invite the visitor to a meeting) – Include venue and time of course.

Send a follow up email campaign. See above.

93. If it worked – YAY!

If the event paid for itself, i.e. you hit your minimum target, then book in to do the next one straight away. The rule is that people often visit the same exhibitions over and over again, and if you are there next time you have a better opportunity to close a sale.

If you did better than your minimum – set your goals higher next time!

Exhibitions work because you usually have a larger concentration of people concentrating on buying services. They are usually 1 or 2 days where you can collect lots of contacts and leads.

Exhibitions are strange creatures in that although you will get leads and sales from the room if you get the mix right, you will often need to do an exhibition more than once to get maximum benefit.

94. What if it didn't work?

Many exhibitions fail to deliver what they promise. You can avoid the worst of theses by doing your homework in advance, finding out the previous year's attendance, breakdowns of footfall etc...

If you do get a disappointing result, find out if the event worked for anyone who exhibited, if not then do not repeat the exhibition.

If it did work for a couple of people find out what they did to make it work, find out if you are speaking to the same people and if you are – try again with a revised plan.

Section 9 – Google Stuff

Much of today's marketing budget goes towards supporting or trying to master this dark art and although there are a lot advantages to PPC campaigns I will always remember this wise adage of one internet marketer.

> *"To be No 1 on Google is easy, just spend 1p more than the competition"*

Pay per click is not for everyone, but it is a very powerful tool that can radically increase your exposure and increase the visitors to your site. There are several strategies that work with Google but like all tools, if you use it wrong then you can break a lot of things – especially the bank!

I am not going to go into a lot of detail here on the subject but I will give some general guidelines; my main advice is to get someone in to do this for you! Preferably someone not in your industry, who does not understand your industry and is going to approach this from the user's perspective.

I recently came across a locksmith whose PPC bill went up by £800 a month but the changes his new supplier made reduced his leads to zero.

In addition, a plumber who was paying £22 per click, he thought his work was coming from Google but when he switched off his campaign – his sales did not change at all.

My second piece of advice is being fanatical about results with PPC – not click-thru's not impressions or page views but hard monetised sales.

Too often people accept traffic as the result of PPC and not hard sales. Results must drive the campaign

95. Google AdWords

Google AdWords campaigns are the central pivot of Google's advertising income and can guarantee your number one position on every search if you are willing to spend just 1p more than your competition.

The downside of AdWords is that if you do not set your target right then you will get a lot of traffic that is not relevant to what you are selling and therefore you massively reduce your conversion ratio. Worse still badly targeted google AdWords can cost you a fortune in cash and reputation.

1) Study Keywords in advance and spend nothing until you are sure you are ready. This is one of the few times I will say doing nothing is better than doing something badly. I remember reading Jay Conrad Levinson saying a bad letter that goes out is better than a perfect letter that

doesn't get sent! That is not the case here.

    a. Long Keywords with low competition – research keywords there are a lot of tools available to help you research, Google has several worth looking at. We have listed some on our website to help.

    b. Exactly relevant keywords – relevancy of keywords is an interesting idea, if someone searches for "Blue Screen of Death" are they really a client for the IT Company? If someone searches for "free online courses" – are they looking for a professional training company? Make sure your keywords are

exactly relevant so that you are not paying for traffic you don't want.
c. Use negative keywords extensively – the best example has been done to death in writing about Google AdWords but it is still the best example – exclude the word "Free" – if someone searches for "free sales leads London" I don't want to pay for them to land on my website!
d. Use Geographic and network options carefully. Remember they are only as accurate as the data that feeds into them. At the moment I am writing this book in east London but the internet connection reports me

browsing from Dresden in Germany!
- i. If you fix boats in London, advertise geographically so that you just get London traffic. If you service nationally then be a little more choosy.
- ii. Don't use display network unless you are using very defined searches, it costs a fortune!

e. Test and Measure
f. Test and Measure

2) Use A/B Testing on Ads – this means don't run one campaign but run two – Google allows you to do this

with their AdWords tool so take advantage of it.
   a. Write two versions of the same Advert changing some element of the ad in the second advert and see which one is the better performer – in terms of conversions.
   b. When you find which advert performs better, create a new version of it with a slight change and do the same thing.
   c. ONE THING: - statistically significant numbers are needed for this to work. If you only get 3 clicks over the campaign there is not enough evidence for A/B testing.
3) Ads have structure – All Adverts have a language and a structure and an appeal –

don't forget that when writing your adverts for Google.

    a. Line One – repeat the keywords so they make sense – asking a question is a great way to do this "are you looking for more sales?"

    b. Line two – Why to click your link Emotional Selling point

    c. Line three – Features and Benefits

96. Google Display Ads

These appear as banners on people's sites and on network sites like YouTube. Sometimes a bit of an odd relevance and sometimes connected to peoples search history they can be quite useful if used correctly.

There are four types of ads you can choose from

- Text ads. The Google Display Network allows you to run the same text ads on display as you would on the search network. Text ads consist of a headline and two lines of text, and allow advertisers to create a range of ads to test which copy is generating the most clicks.
- Image ads. A static image that would fill the entire ad block on the website it appears on. You can include custom imagery, layouts and background colours on image ads.
- Rich media Ads. Rich Media Ads include interactive elements, animations or other aspects that change depending on who is looking at the ad and how they interact with it. For example, a moving carousel of products.
- Video ads. Video ads have become more popular since

YouTube is included on the Display Network. You can now use AdWords to place your ads next to YouTube videos.

The rules are the same as those for AdWords but be careful – these ads appear on other people's sites and maybe even on the sites of your competition.

1) Choose the formats carefully,
2) Define a tight "reach" keywords, geography and subject
3) Test and Measure

97. Search Engine Optimisation

Each page of your website needs to advertise a single product or service, it needs to be worded in such a way that it will appear when your client is searching for you.

In the case of a clothing store that was easy to detect, people were searching for "rain coats for sale" but for you it may be a little bit more complex.

Don't let SEO Gurus confuse the matter. The site page needs to sell just one thing and that one thing is "a raincoat"

- If your clients are searching for "image consultant SE10" then your webpage should use those words approximately 5% of the page content.
- The First Header <H1> Should contain those words
- The Sub Header <H2> should also contain those words
- The Page <Title> Should contain those words
- The Page Body text should contain those words
- The footer should contain those words
- The Google Ad should contain those words
- There should be alt tags with those words on them

- There should be links into the site with those words in the body (approx. 3 – 6% density)
- URLs should have those words in them

I think you get the idea. One single subject optimised page. If you want to, you can also include keywords for the site as well as the page (i.e. how do I get more sales and "telesales")

98. Don't forget Overture

Google are dominant in the search engine arena but do not write off the others in the industry. Often Overture (Microsoft Bing) is cheaper and easier to win. And although there are not as many searches done on Bing, it is worth remembering for many it is still their default web browser home page.

In addition, the competition is smaller so it is easier to dominate than with the bigger competitive pool that is Google.

99. Back links

Back links are links from sites that connect to your chosen web page. They should be specific and relevant and obey the SEO rules above. They are not as important as they used to be but they do still count towards getting you to number 1 in Google organically.

The thing with backlinks is to make sure that they are from relevant and reputable sources or they may even degrade your websites performance.

100. YouTube

Did you know that YouTube is the third biggest search engine? It seems we would much rather listen to a video than read a web page. Although I think it would be useful to check that information against what we know of the browsing habits of different age groups.

One thing that is worth remembering when you put up a video on YouTube is that Google actually transcribes what you say in the video and adds that to the SEO. In other words, what you say is indexed just like written text.

So, when you put up your video, check the transcript to make sure that google "heard you right".

This is brilliant for information products and for reviews etc. However, remember the more you give away free the less the customer will need you.

101. Google Local

Google Local is becoming more and more dominant as Google is striving to make the results that you see more and more relevant to what you are looking for. It is the directory element of the Google search and appears above the natural results.

If you are searching for a locksmith, Google is likely to use your location (using something called GEOIP) to make sure the results it shows you are more relevant.

It is my opinion that this is perhaps the least utilised Google service but the one most likely to bring you in sales. Especially if you are a shop or Restaurant. Advertise your business (for free by the way) on the Google directory.

102. Local Pages & Directories

Free listings on websites like local directories and yell.com can really help move your business up the SEO ladder if they are done right. Consider getting listed in DMOZ.ORG and any other directories that will have you.

Be careful of two things, firstly that the listing is correctly classified and secondly that the listing is accurate.

Make sure the page they point to exists and of course has relevant information – DMOZ for example is very strict about this.

There is a list of directories and search engines on www.hdigms.com/listings

Section 10 – Social Media

The rise of social media and social media advertising make available to the small business some very interesting tools for niche and sector marketing. You can generate well-targeted traffic from LinkedIn or Facebook advertising.

When considering PPC consider your audience, perhaps Facebook is not the best medium if you sell a product Business to Business. If you are selling direct to the consumer, then it can massively increase your exposure and thus your sales.

One word of warning here – I found one client advertising on Facebook but with no test and measure in place – we didn't know if the clients were visiting the website or buying as a result of the promotions.

When we put in place the measuring needed to test this we found the CTR

(Click through Ratio) was as close to zero as made no difference.

103. Facebook Page

Using a Facebook fan page does give you an edge as it provides good trackback links to your site and of course a discussion page for your clients and friends.

It is a good idea to separate your business and personal Facebook accounts to ensure there is no cross over in message or content – you don't really want all your business contacts to know you are playing Farmville (or do you?)

Post links on Facebook using a URL shortener like goo.gl so that you can see how effective the CTR (Click through ratio) is.

Run your banner and text ads to small niche groups and A/B test until you get the best response.

Plan your involvement as an integrated part of your campaign

104. LinkedIn Adverts

LinkedIn has a great Pay per Click advertising service which can be used to market to particular niche concerns.

With linked in ads I would suggest going with the CPC (cost per click) option as safer than the cost per impression. If you find you are getting a lot of business from the clicks then try the per impression method as it may work out cheaper.

The nice thing about LinkedIn Adverts is how tightly you define your audience, right down to the size of company – even company name.

Oh set an end date, that means you have a limited spend, you can always reset it if you need to.

Set a low daily budget to start with – remember though £8 per day is £250 per month!

105. Twitter

Twitter is useful for keeping track of potential clients and leads. In addition, if you use a product like Hootsuite, you can "blast" tweets out on a regular basis.

I think the real power of twitter though is trawling for people asking relevant questions of the Twittersphere, have Hootsuite look out for key questions to which the answer is "buy my service", reply to the tweet directly with some free advice, follow the asker and then start a conversation.

This is very labour intensive and not for the feint hearted, there are other ways to manage this process but once again, it is intense.

Twitter's adds another way to keep in touch with your existing clients and contacts – I always follow everyone I meet and who emails me – they can see my posts and I can see theirs.

106. Pinterest Advertising

Actually quite good for the consumer market, Pinterest allows you to pin a picture or webpage and target who sees it. This is a relatively new idea for this site so it's still test and measure!

Pinterest has many users; the question is really about how you fit this in with the rest of your marketing campaign.

107. Instagram Advertising

Once again quite good for consumer market. Facebook bought out Instagram a while ago and they are being very protective about adverts.

That said cheaper and less competition a true Guerrilla opportunity.

Section 11 - Email Marketing

We are inundated with emails every day and it is easy to write it off. Email marketing is a long way from being dead. It has changed a lot, it is even more important now to make sure that your prospects see information that is relevant to them and their business. A decent email campaign is responsive to the users' actions and responds to their needs without your intervention.

Typically, Email campaigns should form a central part of the marketing mix.

However, control the email campaign from your CRM and marketing automation system and don't use it on its own, like all of the methods here, though it is a powerful tool it is made more so by using it alongside other methods.

108. Newsletter Campaigns

Though I am not a great fan of newsletters, I suspect I have read but a handful in my entire online career, they are better than doing nothing.

One thing they are good at is making sure people know that you are alive and well.

Send your prospects an email once a month, fortnight or week. In that newsletter, make sure there is information that is relevant and useful to them or at least interesting. Don't just talk about what you are doing, use industry news that you think is relevant and possibly even slightly off centre of topic.

All links in the newsletter should be trackable. If you link to someone's site or to a page on your site, you should know who visited the page and what they did. X2 Identity is very good at this and even tracks anonymous traffic.

There should be a simple single clear call to action on your newsletter than the reader can see straight away as soon as they open the email. That means "above the fold" before the need to scroll.

Although the jury is still out, personally I think short emails and newsletters are more effective, they don't confuse the issue and they appeal to the browser instinct in us.

There must be an unsubscribe – but use the unsubscribe to sell more of what you do. I am sorry you are not interested in our newsletter campaign – what subjects are you interested in? May we approach you in the future if we add these subjects?

109. Campaign Emails

A good email campaign specifically addresses an action performed by the prospect and gives the prospect a clearly perceived and definite benefit in exchange for an action.

The Benefit should be clear enough for the prospect to recognise it and perform and desired action (click thru, purchase or phone call).

Email campaigns should be bi-directional communications, never send an email from a "no reply" address. If you send an email to a contact and they click a link that is a conversation. If you send an email to a prospect or client and they delete it, that is not a conversation but a failed broadcast. If a client does not react to your email, then they have told you something!

We want our clients and contacts to interact with us so we can understand what they need; we should always be trying to provoke a response – a clear call to action.

A no is an answer and a useful one, take it away with you (complete with the reason why of course) and rebuild your offering to turn the no, into a yes.

Let me give you an example.

We sent an email to the people we met at the Lambeth Means Business Expo telling them that there was a security issue with a certain well-known browser. (Useful information).

We suggested there was a fix but it depended what type of computer they were using – so we provided a single call to action with two buttons.

Click Below to fix! [MAC] [PC]

We got a reasonable response and we learnt that a percentage of those that responded were mac users.

We then sent the mac users a series of emails about mac security and doubled our Mac Sign-ups!

Campaigns should be specific, targeted and have a definite desired outcome.

110. Email Selling

Emails can be a great tool for selling information products if you can get a good data.

Fashion and habits have changed and change all the time on the subject of whether you should use long sales emails or not. My own experience, short emails work better as they allow the whole message to be scanned in a couple of seconds.

Most important tip here is your call to action. Like all your marketing you must make sure the what, why and when call to action is clear – the clearest piece of information on your page.

I would use a mixture of methods on email marketing; start with informational to get the reader onto a sales website.

111. Nurture Campaign

We have a campaign that we set up a few years ago, the intention of the campaign was to nurture the people we met networking through a proscribed process to the stage where they were "friends" of the business, were willing to take my calls and, if they were in the catchment – buy my services.

Using this campaign helped to increase the number of sales leads we got from networking by about 150% over just a couple of months.

Recently, I launched the Sales Engine, this is a small consultancy which specialises in online and offline marketing for people who sell their knowledge for a living (consultants, trainers, coaches) and I used the Networking MasterPlan Nurture campaign.

In just 2 networking events where I was not the main speaker, not sponsoring the group just around the table I got 10 leads! 3 of those leads turned into fast sales and another 4 turned into sales over time.

Write up a nurture campaign and use it to manage your business relationships with those that you meet networking.

112. Signature Appeal

Does your email signature sell on your behalf? It should do! Try putting a graphic special offer below your signature line on every email you send. On the Sales Engine Website, we have a couple of videos to show you how to do it.

Make sure the offer is clear and up to date but more than that – make sure the image is embedded in the email and does not make the email too large to send/receive. And remember every email gets the offer.

113. Tips Campaign

I have seen this work really well, you have your contacts and website visitors sign up for free "tips" on a weekly or monthly basis. The tips are simple short emails that the visitor can implement themselves. Every 4 tips, send a plain sales email – at the end of a tip! Keep the tip email short – simple and plain and if you can add a video or landing page for it – all the better!

Remember you want the visitor to click a link and interact with you, and you want to know it happened.

114. Can you Help?

People love these emails – especially if helping you is helping them. I recently sent out a campaign email to about 3,000 contacts and got about 80 replies requesting help for a friend who was writing a sales book. (Not this one) We were overwhelmed with the response and of course as the introducer I gained that valuable thing – reputation.

You can't do these too often but once every couple of months is perfectly fine.

115. Blog to Email

There is a formula I once saw that amused me. I am not entirely sure it is correct but it works for a good basis to consider how to fuel your email marketing.

1 book = 9 whitepapers
1 White Paper = 7 Bloggs
1 Blogg = 3 emails
1 email = 5 tweets.

As I say I am not sure this is accurate but it is worth considering the repurposing your materials for each media. Remember back to our first ideas. Message and Media have to be aligned. So you can't just copy and paste the Book to twitter!

116. Buy My Book Campaign

This is useful if sent to your marketing list as a small limited campaign of maybe 3 or 4 emails. Buy My Book campaign is relatively simple – you can add to this but the basics are.

Email 1 – I am writing a book, order your advance copy now and get <compelling offer>

Email 2 – My Book launch party!!!

Email 3 – My book has just been published and I would love you to buy a copy and tell me what you think.

Email 4 – My book is out now, buy yours for <Special Offer>

Before we begin to sell, we need to decide a couple of things. They are important and they will make the difference between success and failure in your marketing.

A lot of these marketing ideas are low cost and some need cost you no more than a little time and effort. You do not need to be rich for this to work, but you will definitely need these three personal qualities working **in** you before these powerful methods will work **for** you.

These three over-arching principles of personal productivity are going to be key to getting sales.

Section 12 – PPPPP

You may have heard of the 5 Ps – Proper Preparation Prevents Poor Performance.

The First Principle of Success – Personal Preparation

You must be prepared; you must have a plan and must be willing to stick at it through the tough times in order to get to the good times.

For years during my first business I just drifted, I did not drive the business in any particular direction, I had no real plan, no real goals and I managed to achieve no real results. Once I set a goal however, I found that it was not only easier to decide what to do – It was incredibly easy to overtake the goal set and move onto the next one.

The first principle of success is to prepare for success, write down a goal and a plan.

Be Prepared – also means making sure you can **deliver success**, whatever you are selling make sure that you have the **capacity** to take on the extra work – don't leave it to chance, but plan how you are going to scale your operation to make room for the extra sales.

> *We were working on a sales campaign for a Local Image consultant and as part of that campaign we had bought a list of 250k names and addresses for an email campaign.*
>
> *The industry standard response rate for email campaigns is on average 0.5% - now if you want to get 10 enquiries a week you need to be sure you are sending 2,000 targeted emails.*

> *This planning meant that: - firstly we did not get smacked by the internet service providers as a spammer and secondly the client – a sole practitioner – was not overwhelmed with sales calls.*
>
> *In addition, we were able to control the flow of leads from this source by increasing or decreasing the number of emails sent. This suited the client really well.*

Be Prepared – What does success look like? Is it 30 sales a month or is it £20,000 a month or more! Setting a proper goal that you are able to measure your performance against. Setting a goal is just like setting the GPS in the car, it's an aid to get you to your destination.

Write down the goal and commit to it publicly, for example write the goal and the progress onto a whiteboard in your office where you and your staff can see it.

Be Prepared – The Radical gear changing in the sales engine model, means that you have got to be **prepared to change your ideas**, be **willing** to be **open minded** and willing to accept **change**. Make no mistake; a **great enterprise** like the one you have embarked on needs **vision and commitment and an open mind**.

The Second Principle of Success – Personal Productivity

Nothing in this life comes without a lot of hard work and success with the sales engine is not going to be an exception to that rule.

> *There is no substitute for hard work*
>
> *Thomas Edison*

Personal Productivity is going to be key to getting this system to work for you.

Personal Productivity – This is all about taking the plan and doing what it says, consistently. Yes – Work on the plan and refine the plan over time to make sure that it reflects what you are trying to achieve in your sales and in your business, throwing away what is not working and embracing new ideas and methods – but keep doing it.

Personal Productivity – There is no magic wand here, your personal productivity, your personal hard work and commitment is what is going to make this work over time.

> *No matter how great the talent or efforts, some things just take time. You can't produce a baby in one month by getting nine women pregnant.*
>
> *Warren Buffett*

Personal Productivity – Time to grow, to extend your skills and abilities and embrace new ways of doing things. Your old skillset is still useful but in order to succeed you are going to need a new way of doing things. You are committing to learning the new skills and doing the training needed in order to make sure that you have the skills necessary to make the sales engine work for you.

I have found that if I set aside a certain amount of time each day to work just on my marketing, I am significantly more productive. Working on my marketing re-focuses my energies on the business and what it is that I am trying to achieve.

Nigel Botterill gave me this idea when I attended one of the Entrepreneurs Circle Weekend events he runs. I found the advice to be very useful!

That daily focus, every day, six days a week (yes six days not seven) will become the focal point of your business, the reminder not to get distracted by "other things" you could do.

Every day my marketing time reminds me about my core focus, what it is that I do that makes my business what it is. It's easy with that constant reminder to avoid getting distracted.

The 30 minutes or one hour I spend daily on my marketing is my personal productivity time and it is that time that makes my business rock.

The Third Principle of Success – Personal Commitment

The third principle here is often overlooked, people try new systems all the time in their attempt to get more sales; and they give up after just a few weeks. Nothing will be achieved if you don't focus on getting the results you want. You can achieve everything if you commit to completing the course.

> *You can only eat a whale one bite at a time – and it takes time and commitment to finish the whale*

Let's take telesales as an example, according to one source of information, 80% of people that buy, buy on the 5th phone call or meeting but most sales people stop at 2 or 3. Personal commitment to follow through is the third principle of success.

Personal Commitment – to see the whole process through the whole six months of this campaign from here on in – your primary focus and commitment is to the sales engine marketing plan that you are going to write.

Personal Commitment – to make sure that all you do in this campaign is done to the highest possible standard even if it takes a long time to get right, you are going to be committed through to the end of the sales campaign.

Personal Commitment – to spend 1 hour a day marketing your business using the tools you pick from this toolkit.

Don't forget you need to test and measure your own performance and be willing to see when you need to change behaviours because your bad habits are clogging up the engine and preventing it from running like it should.

I have to confess, that I am easily distracted and I get side tracked into all kinds of things rather than do what my diary tells me I should be doing. Worse than that, I often find myself trying to buck the system that I PUT IN PLACE!

About a year ago, I suddenly realised that this propensity to push away from what I had planned was a bad habit and one I had to cure myself of.

I created a brand new goal setting methodology called CREATIVE STEPS to help me get from the place of high distraction to high focus in just a few months.

It was essential that I deal with the inherent issues of my own habits before I could even hope to see success.

You can find More information about the CREATIVE STEPS method on the website
www.hdigms.com/creativesteps

Sharif George Always Happy to Help

Sharif George runs a small sales and marketing consultancy called the Sales Engine.

If you need help with any of this, he is more than happy to have a chat and offer up some suggestions.

www.howdoigetmoresales.com

07497713609

---

[i] © The Sales Engine Survey – 150 Coaching Clients questioned over 3 month period.
[ii] Business to Business
[iii] Business to Entrepreneur

www.ingramcontent.com/pod-product-compliance
Lightning Source LLC
Chambersburg PA
CBHW071437080526
44587CB00014B/1880